When
You
Get Older

By Gabriel Gaiusbayode

CONTENTS

Prelude

THE FINE LINE WE WILL WALK

By this time, *You* are old enough. And if I know my family, *You* are starting to ask. . . questions. But not just any ol' questions. The deep ones. The ones on the other side of the pool. The ones that stimulate thought, and if *You* are not careful, *You* will drown. *You* are probably asking questions about love. . . and boys. . . a story for another time—the point is that one night, I thought about ending it all, then I thought about calling *You*. *You* were too young to remember because. . . it never happened, I never called. I knew that it'd be the same routine, leading to the same result of not speaking with *You*. And I needed *You* at that moment. But this isn't your fault. None of it is. Though the moment made me ponder "the question"— what is love? — truth is I'm no stranger to a woman's attraction. No stud, still no slouch. But if a woman said that she loves me, and she's barely seen me, I might think her insane. . .

So
if she
is insane,
and I
barely
see *You*,
what
does that
make me?

Well, in
this story,
we answer
that question,

And by the end of this book,
If *You* do not already know
You will learn,
whether
your Uncle
loves *You*,
or whether
your Uncle
is insane.

A TWINKLE TO DIE FOR

Perhaps we were stars,

from a distance we were beautiful,

and the world forgot we were burning.

I

We Would Be Honored If You Would Join Us

THE NIGHT

We learned in The Night
      your mother,
      my Mother,
      your Father,
      our Father,
      and your Uncles,
formed a circle of anticipation,

This polygon soon
became a heart—
you should've seen it

Did you at least, feel it?
did you feel the Light?

We became Lanterns then.
all lit up with joy,
each of us
a beacon for you,
signals blinking
as lighthouses do.

In that luminous moment,
we each pact for the journey,
and just as the night arose,
so did I.

THE DEBT

And how must I repay him?
how can I?

"The happiest moment of my life,
 was of your Daughter."

So I'll give all that I can,
I'll give him
a hug
and
a promise,

Don't Let Go

HOW DOES WATER BREAK ANYWAY?

These are important questions,
but on a highway
with a car of panicking men
and a pregnant wife,
a kid could probably
pick a better time.

"How can I help?"

That's what a child
is really asking.
important questions.
adults are hard at hearing,
they accept the world
as it is, pretending to know
what they are doing.

I think we are lost. . .
won't say another word.

ARE GUARDIANS ANGELS?

We are raised to believe
our God lives above us.
I too believe in this spiritual compass.
a sound breeze telling me to look up
and read the clouds like our ancestors.
watch these compositions of water
formulate into angels dancing above
the hospitals of newborn children.

Perhaps this celebration is a symbol
of the sky's protection.
though I would be born yesterday
if I forget that a cloud holds rain
— forget that these angels could be storms.

I often look to nature for a sign but
maybe the weather is best left alone.

Best left to God for judgement.

only fifteen trips
yet the sunrise of your birth
made a man of me

SONS OF WINTER

Parents hold the torch,
but life is an avalanche,
unpredictable and often cold.
my parents froze apart,
could say their love was buried
under the snow and the mountain.
your Father raised the torch,
your Uncles carried the mountain.
I once believed this natural disaster
was God giving my family to winter,
or this ice age of an existence
was hell freezing above us.

So maybe I am a shallow stream
to believe this glacier melts.
but new life does feel
like summer and spring,
salvation beneath the welts.

SOL OF THE GROUP

You could've been a Sun,
because you brought us together,
and there's only one thing
at the center of our Solar System
capable of such power,
so, truth be told,
I was convinced that you'd be a Sun.
you could say, I was right.

SMALL FAMILY AMBITIONS

Alchemy is the essence of humanity,
the Son showed that.

Proved that there is a science
to miracles,
and our daily prayer
is someone practicing this principle.

Turning
          a pain into a perspective,
          a funeral into a celebration,
          a loss into an adjustment,
          and like water to wine,
Turning
          A You into a Hope.

DESPERATE ACCEPTANCE

This vigorous love
comes from a void
of what we have lost.

A complex passion
to hold dear what
we scarcely acquire
but are deserving of.

There were no
steps to climb,
broom to jump,
or legislation to sign.

My brother's smile
is all we needed for
your mother to
become my sister.

It was enough.

WATCH THE KID

Some days
>i just watched you.

Some days
>i watched your head tilt,
>your eyes close,
>your tiny right foot warm the left,
>and i would listen to you dream,

>hear you breathing harmony into the room,
>trusting me without even knowing my name.

Some days
>i just watched you laugh,
>and giggle,
>watched you suck your two *whittle* fingers,
>and sprinkle the saliva across the floor,

>breathing joy and grossness into the air as a kid should,
>trusting me to clean up all of your ooze.

Some days
>i watched you cry,
and on these days,
>you taught me everything will be okay,
some day.

CHEERS AND GOOD FORTUNE

New life is a baptism,
where the family is cleansed
and reborn anew.

> From Mother to Grandmother to Iya,
> from Brother to Uncle to Aburo,
> from Husband to Father to Baba,
> together
> we ascend.

Carried on the wings of our little ladybug,
— a baby, that cries from the soles of her feet,
and smiles through the fluff in her cheeks,
this new little sunshine is photosynthesis,
transforming what was once our identity,
To wash our sins away you tried.
but this is only the beginning of a stream,
and what awaits for Sons who dream,

but a table.
a body.
and mead.

THE END OF THE TUNNEL

The Men in our family
led the way,
and they lead the way.

Some may consider this
reality blasphemous,
but only those that
didn't see the world
four boys
had to carry,
the warmth we had to create,
the God we had to find.

So this means one thing,
we made decisions, (as will you)
and we make decisions, (as will you).

         And sometimes
these decisions are   these decisions are
Yellow Brick Road   *Shifting Sand Land*
       nonetheless, we made decisions.

Because leadership is a red light,
a hopeful glow that tells the Bats,
"there is an end to this tunnel"

This is what we learned
from our Mother,
and our Father,
who both gave us two lights,
before we could even fly.

mama sees the clouds
but children of silver lines
play in the rain

REASONABLE DOUBT

Deer often die in the Night
where cars don't stop roaring,
but why shouldn't we
cross the street?

BROTHERHOOD OF BLIND SERVITUDE

God gave us faith,
a hopeful dialect.

      Faith believes in the sunshine
      on a rainy day,
      Faith believes in the Lord's return
      even when He goes away.

Faith
is the murderer of intuition.
Faith
is what killed the boy.

The news said, "it was the sea that swallowed him,"
but I knews better. . .
I knews he never questioned the vessels he drank from,
I knews it was Faith that killed him.

Even when the glass cup was cracked,
even when the liquids turned to dust,
the boy never questioned.

For the boy was Sub-Saharan,
and to a nomad of the desert,
Flint
is paradise.

You don't question paradise,
you have Faith.

FORTUNE COOKIES CRUMBLE

Every night I had the same dream.

There's a woman,
a beautiful woman
       in a blood-stained dress
       with large black spots,
       chain-link bracelets,
       six-inch stilettos,
       and a cloud of smoke
       silhouettes her thick frame.

Somehow, I already know that she's
       a philanthropist,
       a geologist,
       a theologist,
       her name is Jacqueline,
       and she's dead.

We meet in an elevator,
she stands by my left shoulder,
stares into my temple
humming a melody,
a familiar tune,
an AAB lyric,
déjà vu perhaps.
the elevator doors open.

As we prepare to enter the city streets
she steps into a larger woman
       with bricks for pupils
       and a rope for a tongue
       that swallows her whole
       and skips away into the jungle.

My jaw hangs open,
my feet are frozen,
everyone else—
still walking.

The elevator doors
lock me in.
it goes down.
didn't know it could get lower than this.

The fallen beads from
her broken bracelet,
float
inside
of
the elevator,
marching into a message
before my eyes
that read,

> "The Good Men
>   died young,

>   The Bad Men
>   died slow,

>   The Honorable Men
>   lived forever,
>   as they were buried with the young,

>   Welcome to the Jungle."

EVOLUTION OF THE FELINE

It's the little things that adjust our perspective,
like the reality of animalistic evolution,
this optical realization may teach is of an ancient art,
and the oldest art form of this education is survival.
it's how hunters know not to cut fruit from poison ivy,
and gatherers know not to shit in the wrong bush,
for a tiger in nature is just a big cat,
whereas a cat in the house is just a little tiger,
so be wary of how you treat the smallest things,
because though tiny to our eyes,
the bite can kill,
all the same.

MONKEY BREAD

That taste will always be a symbolic moment,
a memory of the communion between strangers,
a reflection of our last supper.

As the bells jingled and
        we drank, *not you*
        and we danced, *yeah you*
and we actually looked like a family that loves each other,
but no one ever prepares for a red wedding.

ASK NOAH. . .

At the end of the day,

      there was Peace,

      there was Harmony,

      there was Grace,

      and there was Love,

      so maybe

God destroyed us.

II

The Autumnal Equinox

A MESSAGE FOR THE CLOUDS

Tell the storm
i will never forget
my brother's ship
was torn to splinters.
fragments ripped
into his lips
as he was forced
to swallow the salt
of an unforgiving wave
that spares no man
daring to love his children.
though we must accept
these disasters as natural,
i will never forgive
a flood willing to kill
somebody's son.

WE DIDN'T LEARN FROM ICARUS

We know Them,
we've seen Them,
children hidden from their fathers,
brothers ripped from their children,
yes— we know Them,
we wrote the eulogies.

Silently we swore to rise above their ashes
until wings began to stitch into our ankles
as we became birds reaching for foreign stars.

Animals clawing to escape the hell we wrought.

There's a reason stars remain distant,
and the Sun, *though it brightens our world,*
knows to stay outside of our atmosphere.

Because on this rock,
nothing is innocent,
nothing is sacred,
nothing is safe,
not even us.
and from a solar perspective
we
are no different
from Them.

flowers were meant to grow.
we were meant to be beautiful.
but you will learn meaning
don't stop no death.

FROM WHERE THE NILE RIVER FLOWS

Perhaps children of denial
become the best doctors.
the nurses of our minds
attempting to free the crazies.
Liberating madness from Arkham Asylum,
as if Gotham is a safer place to be.

"This isn't real!"
"This isn't real!"
"This isn't real!"

Pretenders of knowing truth,
advocates of telling lies,
Hippocratic oath
hypocritical belief?

Perhaps children of denial
do become the best doctors.

AFTER DAWN

A mammal can fly inside of a dream,
an infant can die inside of a nightmare,
terrifying how | R-E-A-L-I-T-Y |
honors this subconscious escapism,
placing Aladdin's ruby
inside the bowels of our scarecrows.

and fly do we indeed,
become flies.

swarming in the shit.

PRAYING TO THE WAREHOUSE

Let's pretend Hell is a real place.
ever just marvel at the what-ifs
of your mind?

Like what if the angels messed up too?
i imagine their days mimic
what we humans call
the warehouse.

So, what if angels messed up too?
What if they put shipping with the receiving
and the receiving with the shipping?
What if?

Now I know this is a serious job,
perhaps no laughing matter,
but only God is perfect,
and Books ain't say nothing about no angels,
     and the 7th proves that He needs rest days,

and my naivete imagines children die on these days—
i'm only sixteen,
and my brother is innocent. . .
see the paradox here?

So God,
let's pretend angels mess up too,
and negotiate terms for peace.

A TRIAL & A TRIBULATION

Have you ever seen
the conviction of a good man?

I hope you never do,
but if so,
know that I am the little boy
in the back,

      sobbing,
      pleading
      and
      screaming
      "he's innocent."

While the judge,
through gavel and fury,
demands strictly
for order.

IGNORANCE IS SUFFERING

Ever had a dream
where you screamed,
but there wasn't a sound?

Ever had a dream
where you cried
and nothing came out?

Where the sonic within is blue,
like a drowning bubble in
your chest that's new.
Well here I prescribe the outer proof:

      your voice box is broken,
      and the fact that no one sees the noose around your neck,
      shows that our biggest problem
      has always been facing
      the truth.

SELF-DESTRUCTING FOR DIRECTION

Honestly. . . I blame intuition and faith,
but who would believe ideologies
could murder a family. . .
y'know
I don't like to think that I was right,
and sometimes making sense
is all we need to make peace,
at least when you don't know the who,
as this gives us power over the what,
so I will prosecute the only thing I control.

me.

superman's greatest weakness
was never the kryptonite,
it was always the magic.

KRYPTON HAS FALLEN

I remember I used to think things were easy,
until my brother couldn't sleep
because the A.M sunrise would confirm one singular fact,
he no longer recognized the smell of his daughter's hair.

I remember I used to think things were easy,
until my brother couldn't sleep
because *You* would be in his dreams
and all dreams come to an end.

I remember I used to think things were easy,
until I feared my brother not waking up,
as bits of his skin fell apart
before my little eyes.

I remember every night like it was my last.

SILENT HOMES

An empty house
is one without Sol,
a family reunion—
nothing without Sol,
be wary of the mage
who darkens sunny days,
only she can rob a people,
only she can steal their Sol,
leaving nothing but the gray.

CONSEQUENCES OF THE RAPTURE

If one day you awake,
without everyone you know,
would you want to stay,
or would you rather go?

It's clear that Armageddon
bears an arduous weight,
but if shouldered for us to carry,
Lord above already sealed our fate.

PAYING UNJUST DUES

Living is a luxury,
that is why you have to "make it,"
and here's the rub—
living can also be bought,
but for a family like us,
we never seem to afford it.

HOW SCARS LEARN TO STAY

Paper cuts the worst.

It was never made to tear,

But like all things of earth,

It finds a way to hurt.

love must not exist
if the greatest man I know
can't hold onto it.

SORCERESS OF MIRAGE

A shame I thought her once "sister,"
when she was only wife.
Even husbands die alone,
the reality check is,
who am I?

Without a letter of love,
a kiss of goodbye,
without even the *side* of a hug,
couldn't even settle for a lie.

We gave our locs for her to climb,
and now our hair's for us to hang.
so let me be the ghost of her dreams,
a closet's skeleton dressed in flames.

Yes— she made a martyr out of me,
cast my faith into a void.
Rescue the women and children first,
so where's the prince to save these boys?

DIVINE STORKS

Perhaps God is a woman,
a scared mother,
stripping child from breast,
dropping babies on doorsteps,
and...
left us.
perhaps God...
left us.

EMPATHY FOR MY MOTHER

How it must feel
for a Mother
to watch her sons suffer.

How it must feel
for a Mother
to learn her love cannot protect a man.

For a Mother,
to find prayers only whispers in a vast library,
and by the time this in-voice is processed,
a Mother
finds herself draped in the apparel
of a hurricane's shadow.

Polluted air
smothers the breast
she once used to feed.
hard to breathe.

Like a monsoon over yonder,
she was riddled by storm,
now she is riddled by stones,
and dead men.

I DON'T GO TO FUNERALS

Imagine going somewhere
to meet someone
who's already gone.

Haven't ya heard?
don't cha' know?
death don't wait for you.

IT FOLLOWS

Love does not want.

it is neither a convenience,
nor a privilege.
Love is an instinct.
like the belly of a famished tiger,
Love is a carnal desire.
a hunger. a burden.

and some of us (*me*)
will run.

sometimes to dine at this table of "Love,"
we must walk down the steps of pain,
amongst traumas framed in our house,
painted faces laughing at our shame.

and some of us (*me*)
will run.

casting spells beneath our feet,
transmogrifying frames into existence—
house photos growing legs,
stepping out of images to haunt us,
becoming a torment we desperately evade,
but it follows.

and we will never stop
revealing our fear,
for it is around the corner,
dragging feet from mud to mud,
through swamp and through desert,
the blisters on our feet are reminders,
the hunt for truth has only just begun,

and some of us (*me*)
will run.

a college campus,
where a broken boy hides,
no one bats an eye.

THAT MAKES TWO OF US

I relate to Batman a lot,
because I'm Batman!
. . . .
b u t   n o   r e a l l y

This is me,
this is what's real,
and the other guy?

i think he died in that alley.

THE RABBIT MUST DIE

If you run fast enough
you'll learn quicker than most.

There is no safe place in this jungle,
nature provides only ultimatums.

So I (like all things) must die,
before I (like most things) are killed.

Only then can an animal thrive,
and the most dangerous survive.

SHIELDS OF TRAUMA RELEASE SHRAPNEL

Attempting to love someone
you do not understand
is like going to college for something
you do not want to do.

Perhaps it will work out,
but optimism can often
deny the truth,
that is what I tell
the lady in my life.

She sees mistakes,
i see red flags,
she sees an apologetic kiss,
i see paper promises,

She sees our love,
i see a broken heart,
she sees a family and us,
i see us torn apart.

ARAL SEA

My lover is a medic,
a fixer to those who are broken,
she does not speak my language,
i bring her to my land unspoken,
i beg her to wear X-rays— physical,
see my heart beat sentiments.
understand the face i wear is true
hug the shoulders around my blues
hear my village scream "river mercy"
atop dried wastelands, we build anew,
see the land as i see,
see the morgue inside me.
my village walks for miles to drink
pouring outward for internal energy.
my mother carries thirst on her crown,
i beg my love to understand
there's no more water
to go around.

FEARS OF FALLING SHORT

When exceptionality is undefined
it becomes a bubble,
easy to pop.

It can mimic flight,
but it's not going up,
it's falling slowly.

It may look like a perfect sphere,
but it's a fragile,
brittle passion.

THE 187TH DAY

My professor asked the class:
"if you had 6 weeks to live
who would you want to see?"

I want to see an audience crying,
as I become a magician,
making myself disappear.

Allowing your mind to forget me,
will you forget me not?
I often wonder if it's easier
becoming a distant memory.
I already feel like I am.

are we now, stranger?
and if your eyes deem us so,
are we now, danger?

THE WORLD IS PURPLE

i find my mind
a rough place to be.
sometimes i leave it
on the pillow.
you could say,
starting my day
with another run.

but the day runs by me.
i'm another zombie dragging
this corpse i call my body
through the horde of children
swaying between life and death.
perhaps we may not think,
but we still feel the weight
of adulthood's ambiguity.
the complementary colors
collapsing.

grown folk used to have
all the answers,
oddly enough now
i'm one of them too,
i think though i do not know.

either i missed this orientation,
or i'm of the many children lied to.
knowing nothing,
though we know pain.
we know it's easier not to think,
still don't know how not to feel.

sometimes i fear i left my mind
stranded on an island,
zombified,
starving,
purple,
dying,
Lost.

PINCH ME

It is indeed a matrix,
a fascinating code,
a complex fact that our bodies
associate pain with reality.

So much so that to leave our dreams
we demand the pressure of two fingers,
to twist our skin purple,
moving us from one soul
to another soul,
and back to reality.

A blind man once called it
the desert of the real.
For what separates the red pill
from the blue pill
is only pain.

Something we cannot touch,
something we cannot see,
but something we know
is real.

We tell children who grow up,
"Welcome to the real world"
as if their childhood
was nothing but a fabrication,
an illusion with no meaning.

All because it was guarded by
happiness & innocence,
which seems only to exist
within our dreams.

NIGHTS OF WONDERS BLAZE A QUIET SKY

Tonight,
I will rest my nape against grassy meadows,
place my head amongst the clouds
beneath the starry skies,
I will close my eyes,
and gaze upon the wonders
of my world.

Wondering
      how tall you have become,
      how many teeth I have missed.
      how large are your *whittle* feet?
      how many days has it been?

Wondering
      if you think about me still,
      if you know about your mother,
      if you remember who I am,
      if you're wondering about us too.

I will then wander into day,
just as I wandered into night.
Awakening into the next responsibility,
left to wondering what you have become.

WINTER SOLSTICES IN MY DREAMS

The Sun does not rise.
this Sun never sits.
it glares upon me with a somber shine,
engulfing my flesh in radiant gaze.

Where the stars were once far,
they now neighbor reddening eyes,
energy rays pierce my skin— conveniently,
warming what was once a cold body.

Gravity was a weight but now, she is a pull,
I float into horizons within space,
float into Sun until I'm blind to her beauty,
my vision will flee but another sight awakens.

New life will burn within my heart,
like the love of a mother for her son.
am I, to be reborn?
scaled and clipped.
am I, to be forged?
as a knight's sword burns upon iron,
what am I, to be? or what am I, too?
if I, am to be reborn? will I, not die in two?

I comet back to my world,
puzzled and confused,
branded upon my chest
glows a painful blistering black light,
only to be seen from
another's point of view.
something has awakened.

I'M NOT CRYING

when i stub my toe.
i find the rainbow in the sky,
imagine we are dancing to blues,
as the world fades to black.

ADVENTURE STARTS IN THE WASTELAND

The snowflake of anew will butterfly onto my palm,
remind me that shivers ripple from head to toe.
a moment when conscious feeling returns
with chills that remind us of our desire to be alive.

To be alive is a desire,
a subconscious action,
like a dream
when we dare to dream.

This is the value of reunions,
anticipation is the morning sun,
warm as a husband's kiss,
radiant as a child's smile.

We are hopeful creatures
when we discover love,
we are beautiful humans
when we dare to feel.

UNFORGOTTEN

More than two
too many weeks,
but the day finally came,
and yes— *I was afraid.*

Afraid that you were like me,
afraid that you had. . .
      forgot my face,
      forgot my smell,
      forgot my smile,
      and forgot me.

Over the Atlantic
eight years had passed,
and I. . .
      forgot my father's face,
      forgot my father's smell,
      forgot my father's smile,
      and forgot my father.

I thought we lost you,
but your spirit still curled up
in your father's chest.
you were taken
but *You* never left.

      And I was guilty,
      for what did I do
      with this freedom,
      but betray your memory.
      I left,
      and now
      I—

III

I Think I Hurt Someone

RECOVERING MY TRACKS

Not all things happen for a reason,
but there is a reason for all things that happen.

The effect does not always have a cause,
but there is always a cause to the effect.

A wolf that hunts
three little pigs
is never random,
neither an act of merit
nor heroism.

Sometimes,
big bad wolf
just had
a bad day.

THE PRICE OF RETRIBUTION

Hate
is a deal with the devil.

And no matter
how precious that moment seems,
how smooth that closure feels,
how good that glory tastes,

In the end,
we all learn,
he never picks sides.

scorch my heart within the fire
then tell me to love again.

BREVITY TASTES LIKE A BISCUIT

My love is undercooked,
squandered, and unprepared.

My love looks flavorless
when one spoils
the ingredients of my joy.

I am a golden, frozen,
honey-filled biscuit
baking in an oven
for not enough time.

Yet I am expected
not to be bitter,
not to be stale,
not to be dry.

I AM SICK, MAYBE DYING

Sometimes you'll push me,
wanting to play,
though I won't move.
on rare occasions, you'll call,
having something to say,
but I've become mute,

If love is to feel this. . . microscopic,
like experimental bacteria,
the line between
happiness and anguish
looks like a petri dish,
convoluted in appearance,
toxic in nature.

It is killing me slower than
rats inside prisons of discovery,
animals tested for the survival
of another species,
i may be destined to share this cage
with survivor's guilt—

expect smiling to become strange,
and laughing to become scarce.

To talk and to play is
no longer within my nature.
I may not survive this test.

ACID REFLUX

i love you

       sour milk from a mother's breast
       dripping atop my lips.
       scared children we are
       when instinct cast irons
       into a silver dagger.
       i've grown a sharp tongue,
       hammered and bludgeoned,
       a cutting pain in the throat,
       bringing clots of sunflower's blood
       to the ends of our necks.

i love you

ARTHUR

I carry a balled fist in my left pocket.

Holding onto nothing but lent,
and
air,
and
sweat that moisturizes the lent,
and
sweat that moisturizes my broken knuckles,
dampening the clinch.
like saliva washing against my gums,
what room is left to fill my pockets?
There is none

Not an inch of room to fit a penny,
yet somehow
I am slowly losing change.

MY SHADOW IN THE DARK

Freedom and Chaos.
one set of twins,
often confused.

For one twin
favors new life,
the other,
favors the dead rising.

> through forms of possession
> and conjuring of something,
> not malevolent,
> nor benevolent,
> but something
> that certainly
> isn't free.

Remember the last time you blacked out?
. . . yeah. . . me neither

it took one strike
and i became the storm,
the thunder between madness

THE BRO/KEN POINT

There comes a point
in time— a nanosecond,
a precise moment where you
and the air particles around you
realize that
you
are broken.

A shadow of your former self
still chasing the light.
lost in the possibility that
you
are better.

Better than the thoughts telling you to
                              Walk
                          Down
                              The
                              Steps
                              And
                          Bring
                              Home
                              More
                              B
                              o
                              d
                              i
                              e
                              s

DIMMER SUNS POUR THE NIGHTINGALE'S CRY

I have eclipsed faith,
becoming the Nightingale of my deepest dreams,
embracing the Summer's harvest,
sown amongst my ribs between.

The crescent flows within my vein,
no longer waiting for the right time,
no longer waiting for death to call,
for the song of the soul was born to fly.

Now up, up, and away I goes,
to where I will blind a burning sky,
and mornings that dawn will never come,
the world will know, Nightingale's cry.

For when the blind look upon me,
they will learn vengeance was never mine,
it was merely a loan I was bestowed,
and return this fee I must oblige.

A COLD STEEL

Better thoughts should
accompany the word
"audacity."

It's as if the statement
is a reminder to be still,
because motivation is a spring,
sad part about this concept
is us.

We
are the bullet
and we
are the spring,
both trying to resist
the gravitational pull
of the trigger,
a temptation where life
becomes a wheel to steer.

Though the drive
may lead to dead ends
behind this muzzle,
these conduits of momentum
have the power to move me
farther
away from the ones
i would die for.
i would kill for.
it seems these mechanisms when
put together is really a shovel.

made for two graves.

A MESSAGE FROM THE OTHER SIDE

There's blood on my hands,
there's blood on the leaves,
there's blood on the land,
there's blood on the sea.

my family is drowning,
in all of my dreams,

but I'm standing on water,
for my hands they reach,
i extend my fingers,
the farther they sink,
the louder I scream,
the harder I breathe,

there's blood on my hands,
there's blood on the leaves,
there's blood on the land,
there's blood on the sea,

my family is drowning,
in all of my dreams.

I came here for freedom,
this freedom ain't free.

THE BEAUTY OF FORGETTING

There's a beauty in forgetting,

Forgetting the traumatic experience we call birth,
        forgetting the traumatic experience we call life,

        forgetting how difficult it was to breathe,
        forgetting the cries squeezing our little lungs,

        forgetting ignorance— the inability to walk,
        forgetting that growth hurts your knees too,

        forgetting your heart's lost virginity,
        forgetting the dread, the break, and the sorrow,

        forgetting the responsibility that drags you from rest,
        forgetting dreams and nightmares that plague you,

        forgetting to despise what you look at every day,
        or forgetting to even look into the mirror,

        forgetting reflections hold what you are,
        not what you could be,

        forgetting what you could be, taunts who you are,
        forgetting what you are, mocks what you could be,

        forgetting to bring sorrow with you into the classroom,
        forgetting you woke up sorrowful again,

        forgetting sadness rests on your hip,
        forgetting, forgetting, and forgetting what we forgot,

This amnesia feeds the desire to forget who we are,
becoming the animals that we were meant to be,
the territorial killers lurking inside,

Perhaps my freedom is in forgetting. . .

FRANKENSTEIN'S DREAD

Walked through the produce aisle,
noticed an adorable child.

She was the size of a buttercup,
delicate and precious.
as kindness set on my heart,
I waved a hand of protection.

But what did she see?
danger?
perhaps,
a monster?

Her face curled away,
her eyes fled the scene,
I looked upon the freezer glass,
and whaddya know...
it was me.

On my way home
there was a brother,
a dog,
and a daughter.
Observing with
insecure eyes,
thought to myself,
a beautiful family

Smiled at the dog,
smiled at the daughter,
smiled at the brother,
to my surprise
he began to scowl.

His face began to clinch,
his pupils gunned at me,

but what did he see?
danger?
perhaps,
another monster?

As I looked in the rearview mirror,
and whaddya know...
it was me.

In the evening I walked my mother,
sharing a lovely night,
when I noticed a brother approach us,
internally, I prepared to fight.

The brother noticed my mother,
then he noticed me,
as my face began to still
my eyes pierced his soul.

But what did I see?
danger?
perhaps the monster
others would see?

As I looked into
my mother's eyes,
and realized

it was me.

THE WOODEN SPOON

it wasn't a straw,
it was an over-stepping stranger,
a wooden spoon,
a confession,
a red bottom,
and our little girl,
that made this camel,
almost kill a man.

burn the forest.
look around.
watch how cold you feel.

I AM THE JINCHURIKI

There is no demon on my shoulder,
I must take responsibility
for the horrors I whisper to myself.
the things I tell myself that I do not mean,
the thoughts I have that make me vomit inside,
the pain that I feel.

It is not on my shoulder,
it is inside of me.

Today,
we detox.

true mothers show us
the highest love goes through pain.
push. . . push. . . push. . . push! PUSH!

DETOX I. EVENING SHOWERS

Sit outside alone,

Observe the meteors fly
through the scope of your eye,
find shelter in the bosom of the Earth,
as we are just a twinkle in the Universe.

The moonlight illuminates our lives,
requesting only the truth lying under the night.
this truth—
we are
the light
to the stars

Sit outside alone,

There is comfort awaiting,
coming to mend your crying soul.

As our tears kiss the ground,
the clouds will never forget
to sweep up the pieces we drop,
cleaning up our mess,
then through the darkness,
preparing the skies for mourning,

Forcing the world to cry with you.

DETOX II. CONFRONTING SHAME

Fear will dress you,
shearing your pain into fur garments,
or fear will strip you naked,
leaving you for the winter.

Fear makes men prey
of their own reality,
turning into pale rabbits,
running from their pain.

But under the expensive clothing,
fabrics can never hide the blemishes on our skin,
we can never find shelter from our faces.

Seek out the mirror in your home,
find the pimples on your cheek,
become face to face with you,
make peace with your reflections.
fear runs deep,
eventually it suffocates,
under the coverings in which you hide,
eventually stripping you
beyond nudity,
stripping you
down to the blood
and down to the bone.

DETOX III. THE BASEMENT & THE ATTIC

The leaves are falling,
it is time for us to move.

Upstairs you will find your history,
downstairs you will find
things that no longer fit
into the now.

Both rooms
trying to find room
in our bigger room.

Our past will live forever,
it is the delicate antique
that must receive tender care
when packing our luggage.

Everything under the house has roots,
a horde of seeds that've grown into
a beanstalk of cobwebs we forgot
to tend in the wake of our storms.

This is okay.

I say learn from Mother Earth,
she knows how to prepare for the cold,
she knows her daughter Autumn best,
Autumn knows some things must go.

The leaves are falling,
it is time for us to move.

DETOX IV. OVERCROWDING

If we treat our thoughts
like people,
maybe
the world would be better off,
knowing that there is a place
for the strangers
God forgot to fix.

tell yourself what is
or become lost in what could,
hemlock, the final elixir.

BETWEEN ACTION & THOUGHT

You. Are. Trying.
24 hours. 1440 minutes. 86400 seconds. Your ears are cleaning the wax that will autumn leaf onto your shoulder / your stomach is polishing the heavy pieces weighing you down / the air in your lungs are pushing you forward and exchanging its existence for the sustenance of your life / your skin pores will cry if it's too hot and the surface will harden if it's too cold / your body will tell you the day must end / these things take time / you are trying / so stop trying to try something that your body is already doing / the cries / the growls / the scowls / the run / the stillness / the amnesia / the reason / the dread / just STOP / *You. Are. Healing.*

IV

Our Quest Against Time

FEELS LIKE A WINDOW'S CLOSING

Your Grandmother,
my Mother,
your Uncle,
my Brothers,
your Father,
our Father,
You.

Everyone is trying
to figure this out.

How to love under a clocktower,
whether experiences we dream of exist beyond the window,
beyond the sleepless nights. . .
and where do restless dreams go anyway?

Perhaps making peace with time
may awaken our love.
If so, a question arises this morning—
how does one mourn a dying dream?
Who writes the eulogy for these
nocturnal tragedies?
How do you make peace with time?
The most brutal of constructs.

Your Grandmother birthed Yoruba children. all sons.
it's custom for our babies
to ride their mother's back,
each of us wrapped in cultural cloth,
made home on my mother's back,
she hoped each of her son's children (like You)
could also make a home on grandmother's back.
Eventually, you will get too big,
maybe, she will get too old,
if so, where will this dream go?
My mother, now stares out of a window

The Singing Uncle learned words through
the symphony of flashcards,
melodies atop a rhythmic lap are loud,
they bounce throughout eternity.
harmonizing an adult's nostalgia.
This soundboard is where legacy and love overlap,
an idea of sharing sounds from past lifetimes.
Maybe you will get too big,
maybe he will get too old,
if so, where will this dream go?
My brother, now stares out of a window

Your Father gifted me the best birthdays,
all night sensations of pizza-flavored parties
with friends that would kick-it till dawn—
perhaps the true present was eternal relationships.
My friends and I
still kick-it till dawn.
just as time takes away a man's body,
time gifts his mind with larger creativity,
so I wonder what celebrations
are in store for you...
were in store for you.
Most likely, you will get too big,
perhaps, he gets too old,
if so, where will this dream go?
Your Father, now stares out of a window

As for me, I still dream,
they're much quieter,
soft-spoken imaginations.
I was the youngest in the family until You,
never quite understood why adults do what they do,
but beneath the clocktower of life
we are all required to grow,
soon to be haunted by ghosts of our dying dreams,
and today, I finally understand the adults.
I too, Your Uncle, now stare out of a window.

BONDING & BROKEN THINGS

Brother, do you trust me, or anything greater?
fate for us has been anything but safer,
The Night we believed in destiny sealed our doom,
burying us in a tomb beneath the equator.

Now I fear the proximity of I & your Sun,
yet I request for her time one on one,
we've never shared a day together,
in excitement I fear our moment has come.

Here is the itinerary, locations, and times,
we won't be too long, or too hard to find,
so I beg that your blessing protect our joy,
for in past our glee has been treated as crime.

NO AMUSEMENT IN THIS PARK

It was never the roller coaster.

Not the loops & the pivots,
or the rumbling in our tummies
generated by aerodynamic wakes.
as you can see the others are laughing.

It is the wager,
the blackjack,
the chance that today
one screw is too loose,
two bearings too rusted.

It is the clouds of gambling angels,
the smoked dice on red velvet
poker tables laced beneath golden trims,
stacked chips embroidered with our names—

It is the possibility that we are the odds we ask,
that beautiful weather can be spoiled
by the velocity of our rain dropping bodies.
it is the speculation of what will go first. . .
our minds or our jaws?

It is the question of whether
we are the one screw too loose,
two bearings too rusted,
or perhaps,
the wrong day
and the wrong time.

It was never the roller coaster.

INFANTS OF OLD

Strange times
when love looks
a lot like Bambi,

The shaking deer
still crossing
and coping,

But time teaches us
that loss can be a
ligament of our lives,

A left leg
limping on
shaky turf,

As we stroll
like babies
waddle,

We fall
until
we can stand,

Venturing towards
the sunrise one day
by another day,

Learning that
all lights do not
have to be headlights,

Learning
how to
Walk.

time abides by rules,
laws which can wave like oceans—
surf's up

A HARE'S REDEMPTION ARC

I'm aware that we should,
but just like you,
we can't slow down.

Our eyes meet only two sunrises every week,
a trigger springing us into two a day activities,
our race against lost time

Funneling enthusiasm into this hourglass,
we share gifts from missed birthdays,
exchange stories under a star's gaze,
we play games until the moon is weary.

Another 187 days?
we never know how long "next time" will be,
or if there will be a next time,
so we sprint,
we dash,
we hurdle over exhaustion,
persevering through our regrets.

And I know. . .
I know we should cut our losses,
I know that we should stop.

But it's as if my brakes were gone,
and just like you,
we can't slow down.

ICEBREAKERS WITHIN HOURGLASS

Let's play a game of hide n' seek,
I'll close my eyes, count to ten.
Don't run too high, or too steep,
here is a game we both can win,

                    Let's play a game of hide n' seek,
                    like recess on those summer days.
                    Above the flowers, under the trees,
                    when I catch you, you can run away.

Let's play a game of hide n' seek,
leaving crumbs for me to follow.
You whisper melodies in soles of feet,
this music I'll sing with birds tomorrow.

                    Let's play a game of hide n' seek,
                    embedded in this period of time.
                    I'll share with you what you share with me,
                    deep in our hearts, the secrets we will find.

THE SORROW OF FORGETTING

Reminders hold fast to my shoe,
plant my shins deep into Earth,
as I become a tree of my Mother,
forced to watch pieces of me fall.

"I am dying slowly," is a strange fact,
though we must accept beautiful tragedy,
I exchange dread with ignorance, for peace,
yet reminders are stubborn & plant me deep.

No one ever truly moves on,
skeletons aren't born, they are becoming,
like weeds within the botanist's garden,
when left ignored and unkempt.

Death is in the closet!
reminders are the stench,
the smell of burning biomes,
within a matrix of artificial roses.

For me to uproot my legs
I mustn't deny this truth,
though acceptance of time is no end,
the impermanence always births regret.

This "truth" is the sorrow I carry,
the reminder when I look into your eyes,
I sometimes forget that you're Seven,
in our last chapter, you were only *Five*.

NEVER TOO OLD FOR STORIES:
'THE KNIGHT'S FIRE'

I know a boy that lost both parents,
and under a night's fire, they scorched.

Some boys become men,
but this boy had something to prove.

He desired to show himself sane to the world,
evidence his lost parents were forged, not burned.

A belief fueled by fire and brimstone,
that there's few of us who walk dragonborn.

Thus, from midday to the dusk of night,
he held a tall candle in his grasp.

Watching the wax cry into his palm,
turned his wrist into bubbles of charred skin.

Man screamed *the night* fire's welp,
watching his hand glaze with cherry colored pain.
"This is not supposed to be happening,"
words sound like his knees hitting a deaf Earth.

A dark epiphany suddenly awakened his withheld tears,
as he began to contemplate the singular truth.

He is still a boy learning that Santa Claus is mere myth,
and truth be like gravity to the shoulders of shattered beliefs,
"Bury me deep." he begged in torment,
Bury me deep.

it's been a long night,
but keep on reading,
the sun will always rise

FAMILY TREES PT. I

I believe trees
choose the ground in which they grow,
despite a snowy tundra, they dig their roots deep,
growing a thousand lifetimes— *atop faith*, denying fate.
Perhaps you build like the tree, despite snowflakes
that endanger your feet,
you dig your roots deep, growing a lifetime
atop faith, perhaps, You chose us.
Sometimes family trees can be cruel,

I'm certain you know of this danger,
Abusing that which they should love,
Destroying themselves,
Becoming,
forest fire.
And yet,
we still smile like the tree still grows,
despite time lost in a winter void,

|| still || laugh over Uno cards || play fight & play games || eat together
before we snooze || or simply discuss the day || we be still || doing things ||

Perhaps time isn't codependent with love.

101

THE MIND IS THE TREASURE

I know boys can be edgy,
a bit "crazy" perhaps,
but watch them closely.

A boy only knows so much,
which is how (us) boys are taught,

we aren't given the schematics of life,
we're just given
Legos.

That's where we show what we're made of,
       not on the field,
       not on the court,
here,
amongst the pieces,
is where a boy is made.

WALK

See Dorothy. . .

Memory lane wasn't built on yellow bricks,
my roads are black and concrete.

Young souls rest
beneath the cement,
and mothers of their moonshine
never sleep.

There are no emeralds here,
no gardeners to water
the roses between
these broken sheets.
and potholes imprinted
on sacred ground,
pay no respect to
these weeping streets.

But when I put my ears
to the surface,
I can still hear the rumbling
of Jacob's laughter,
children smiling,
Billy hurdling speed bumps,
we young alchemists
turning gravel into gold medals.
so many moments gone with the wind,
yet I can still hear our wings flapping,
our spirits flying.

As if memory lane was built on yellow bricks,
as if our roads weren't black and concrete.

ETHEREAL OCCURRENCES

My past is my present,
this gift bears no price,
no unnecessary cost,
it can't be bought
or bargained.

it is earned

It is the one thing
that is truly mine,
it is a seed
of my loins.

I only share this child
with those that I love,
who may have come
towards the end
and deserve to know
where I came from.

TOYS ARE US

I dropped a toy's story
into our bucket list,

not because

        I'm your favorite deputy,
        though I am,

not because

        I love you to infinity and beyond!
        though I do,

but because

        in moments when we're apart,
        I want you to remember
        you got a friend in me.
        'cause you do

HOME WHERE YOU CAN JUST BE

Speak freely.
Speak freely when it's happy,
Speak freely when it hurts,
Speak freely when the itching won't stop.

Speak freely when you're curious,
Speak freely when you're wrong,
Speak freely when you speak to us,
Speak freely even when you miss *her*.

Speak into the walls,
Speak into the mirror,
Speak into yourself,
Speak until you speak easy.

Speak like we are your ears,
listening before you speak,
hearing before you think,
Speak because here is not there.
Speak like here is Home.

LIFE'S FULL OF CIRCLES

When you ask for my age, I joke.
I tell you "I'm 85,"
strangers often believe I'm 30,
sometimes methinks I'm 24,
but the truth is

—(I am 23)

The term "growing up fast" floats around often,
I find more kids inheriting adult responsibilities every day,
children surviving and thriving on their ability to adapt,
       daughters raising their mothers' household,
       sons working graveyard shifts to save an addict,
       your Father leaving school to raise me,
       in the absence of our parents, at 19,
       he became "Dad" — *growing up too fast.*

—(I am 23)

These circumstances are born from particular scarcity,
teaching the youth to thrive upon necessity.
sometimes we'll live too fast, dying too soon,
little rabbits racing the tortoise of time— *it follows too.*

—(I am 23)

Maybe hard lessons whooped me wiser than most,
       but metabolism slows,
       responsibility grows,
       people become variable,
over time, too little too late, people change.

—(I am 23)

And
I'll only be 13 once || a time when smiles did not come with a price,
I'll only be 17 once || a time of writing poems for prom dates,
I'll only be 18 once || a time when I was a fresh face in a new place,
I'll only be today once ||
A time when I often remind myself to slow down. . .

—(I am 23)

the seasoning's gone
but at a dinner table
we only need us.

FAMILY TREES PT.2

Time is a mandate,
love is a choice.

It is the exodus,
the "letting my people go,"
it is a blind man returning home,
it is a parent's embrace after your crude day.
Love truly is
the faith and
the finding.

Maybe other families live as beautiful gardens,
but I believe trees choose the ground in which they grow,
I believe these bonds are rooted deeper than seeds.

	it shakes the Earth between our toes	
	it seeps into the hearts of our dearest friends	
	it can come alive on the pages of books	
	and it can even outlast a lifetime	

Maybe other families live as beautiful gardens,
but I believe this love is built differently,
built like the tree,
I believe this love lasts longer.

V

Truth & Reconciliation

and i believe a mother
that gives her daughter to winter
never knew how to love

THE MOTHER & THE MAGE

Stars glisten
before their final dash,
heaven's hand rips open
a womb/an's belly,
stitches \ knits \ quilts
God's power laced into tummy.
holy is the mystery,
babies are the magic.

So let's call a Mother— a Mage if you will,
Her transmutation binds
| a body & a soul |
tying memories into a form,
and continuing the circle of life,
for to move forward yang must be silent,
and her spell must scream *"Push"*
as the world is gifted a new life,
and a woman learns God's language.

But can evil coexist with blessings? Perhaps this is the becoming of a Mage,
for all we know—
> [fire tomes] blacken your palms up to your wrists,
> [conjuration tomes] dampen the human soul,
> [frost tomes] chill a pumping heart,
> But [life's tome] . . . has always been a question mark?
which makes me wonder,
what is the mental toll of bringing new life?

It's often taboo in this culture
to question the sanctity of a mother,
but I've seen the Brendas,
I've bedded the Delilas,
and I've met your mother.
So I will ask the question,
and you must discover the answer—
Who condemns these mothers that abuse their magic?
And can God's power corrupt?

HOW FAMILIES CRIPPLE YOUNG FAITH

Corners are a cage
ants tend to find.
six legs heavy they weigh,
shivering under the cave.

Eight legs roaring thunder,
eight eyes glimmer in the dark,
eight beats a heart per second,
a dark hunger under the moonlight,

Ants desire warm freedom
though corners are a cage
from the eight eyes over the cusp
"pray," says the Spider,

Ants cry.
as rain falls downstream,
the monster outside hushes her scream,
"pray," says the Spider,

Ants want to live free,
to walk as God meant us to be,
is it wrong or unholy to dream?
"pray," says the Spider,

So many can adjust our circumstances,
so many have the power to change,
your mother could have stopped it all,
but "pray," says the Spider.

EMPATHY FOR MY BROTHER

A quiet rage ended the summer,
winter shoulders now brood
falling as dog ears do.

My brother sleeps heavy,
one breath tripping over another,
again— sleep always sounds so close to death.

I imagine his dreams brutal,
splattered catapulting corpses
of those who wronged his daughter,
buried lives under burning homes,
the closer to hell, the better

Wine colored splashes
drench his lengthy hair,
sudden freedom awakens,
his little princess
curled in his arms,
marching into a glimmering light.

As the two leave a burning nest,
I imagine his dream ends here
on the embers of a blissful illusion.
With his daughter,
without consequence,
without suffering,
without his certain death.

Between us— this pain is rarely spoken,
the smoke from your Father and I's shared grievances
always leave one of us choked up.
though when time permits for us to speak,
I swiftly learn my empathy lacks creativity,
His pain— unimaginable.

again the clouds will play
as if your life is a game,
but we have changed

SILENCING THE BELLS

We came in *the Night*.

Delivering a wishlist to the others. Those who stole the star from our tree. 'Twas like awakening beneath the Sun, a bat's first flight out the cave, my eyes bled looking at them, staring into the hearts of *the others*. I remember their paralysis, fear gripping their throats, as we made our way up, marching through black ice. Their dilated pupils quivered. . . I don't believe they expected a Man to have a Family, as if the *monkey bread* was a foreign dream.

See our little girl or deliver a message, one of these would come to fruition on that shivering, silent Christmas, as rage and focus kept us warm. Our shouts challenged cruelty, our fury debated moral hypocrisy, today I learned the gut punch to a coward is a truth they cannot outrun— literally outmanned, figuratively outgunned. My right eye caught a prayer's glimpse, a subtle wisp from my mother's lips, the ground rumbling beneath your feet was a family fighting to see our sweet.

The journey home was long, sometimes
I wish I remembered those weren't people—
       wish I remembered *The wooden spoon*,
       wish I remembered *The broken point*,
       wish I remembered. . . the violence.
I wish upon a shooting star, but there are no stars this Christmas.
Perhaps there is a *beauty in forgetting.*
       any piece of love that lingered in my heart
       any ounce of reason or benefit of the doubt,
       froze on *the other's* doorstep that night.

Though anger bubbled beneath my veins,
a childlike smile filled my face,
Santa got the message.

WE PASSOVER NEBUCHADNEZZARS

The world doesn't need any more silence,
obscure justice is quiet enough.
let the wolves howl under moonlit skies,
a nocturnal reminder for the sheep—
every ounce of digested grass is a breath of grace,
every minute with the sun— a second of benevolence,
every communion is truly a blessing
given from the jaws of my wolf's teeth.
Hear me—
Grace is a verb,
and there is power in a humble hunger.

God knows another world exists,
where the flock is torn apart.

recognize the mustard-seed
within our struggle,
we were born to move mountains

DROWNING THE NIGHTINGALE

Behind every mask
is a face,
smooth cheekbones
and indefinite expression.
Behind every mirror
a man's wishing,
praying to be more than
hollow reflections
and imperfection.
To be more than Me. After all,
I've crippled relationships,
planted red lights on roads
I should have traveled.
I've been the cold wind
and the desert's fury
wrapped in tumbleweeds,
some dry. but never really there.

I've been an ebony phoenix,
a dark umbrella,
a hidden figure
beneath shadows of doubt. fear. and wrath.
I do hope one day courage carries my feet
centering above the abyss of waves,
this shadow of an ocean
where I can bury *the Nightingale.*
Every wing, every talon, and every egg,
watch him fall like an angel,
fading into eternal darkness,
freeing me from obsession.
No longer fighting yesterday or tomorrow,
no longer fighting a mirage born from a thirst
this bruised sea could never quench.
Life must be more than anchors on our feet,
more than the burdens on our faces.

SLEEPING IN THE DARK

Black nights,
a shadow's imagination,
becoming everything,
yet hidden from everyone.

Some ambitions are terrifying to share,
so I listen to the monsters beneath,
with hushed eyes my ears begin to speak,
collaborating with an obsidian Genesis.

Another Ark over a blind sea,
my inner child drowned on the seabed,
eternally rested under the beach,
but the body washed up naked shores.

Hearing the still water whisper,
we dream with our eyes closed,
under the covers of night,
my home is my home.

> No torches,
> cold candles,
> we're children
> of the bold shadow,
>
> Not quite loved,
> though a new moon rises,
> Not quite lost.

AN ABANDONED LIGHTHOUSE CRIES

I'm much better now
but a man still fears,
sometimes I have to tell the mirror
That's okay too.

Imagining my darkest seeds
of the fear I bury under graveyards—

an abandoned lighthouse
a familiar building. paint faded and translucent. the light is dead.
can still hear the metal rub. sounds like rusty hands ticking on
the clock. waves crashing. weeping water whipping dry rock.
seagulls sing the blues. tenor, over the crescendo of black water. rising. *All
Hail Rain!* the thunder lisps. grumbles as the belly of a beast. I sees the
whale tail sparkle when lightning flashes twice. a whispering spotlight. a
storm's divulgence. the birds feast on dead carcasses. unknown. "stranger,"
I tell my trembling mind. recite to drill sergeant the message. god knows
all, but not the faces on the wall. paintings of recognizable shipmates.
worn and torn through concrete halls. bastards to the infants they once
were. monsters to the memories past. a shame. a tragedy. if I stare too long
the floors begin to creak. the blinded lanterns squeak. I think to a God
behind the clouds to pinch me. something does. Pinch me. something.
floorboards begin to creak.

A man still fears—
the stopping light,
the endless raindrops,
from residual effects of lightning's last strike.
A man still fears
the ticking tock,
the little pinch of sanity
where the ocean snapped

and nothing was the same.

RUSH

Scarlet is a bird's color
a feather made of cherries
picked from *Sapele's* trees
falling on the wings of gravity
painting the air a crimson Kool-Aid,
juice-stained graffiti
turns and unseen formation of electrons
to descending glitter
painted sugar riding antigravity
blood cells escaping the vein of man,
our fall from grace
palm pressed to liquid
slushing wall to watermelon seeds
alchemize faint shadows polka dotting
patterns of the ladybug's fortune.
a crystal baptism —
through a savory-sweet peninsula
if dropped a horde of ants solicit.
"treasure the ruby
not the sapphire,"
says the graverobber.
scarlet is a bird's color,
a cardinal's imagination
hence this sugar rush,
shaken up and bottled in
patiently on the edge of a tree
after the fern, certainly
before the bloody daisy
drips a tear for their sacrifice
one day the sky will blush
apologizing to the sons and daughters it eyeballed
and didn't save from the Earth's sweet tooth
now babies learn to walk crawling out fossil-fueled cavities.
children who forgot to weep

now bare garnet shaded faces
while the lucky ones learned to wear *scarlet*
like the ladybug takes to the sky.
in search of a new world,
a better ecosystem,
beyond the chaos of
humanity's transgressions,
rising above our trauma.
I write this to my niece,
my child of blood and sugar,
my little sister of scarlet blues,
and descendant of love and agony,
you are not alone.
Let the lesions of my
words breathe into the
shoulders of spring leaves
and carry this message
of empathy through
the wilderness in strange lands,
giving a missing child shelter before
the leaves begin to fall,
again.

DEAR RAPUNZEL

Your hair is too stubborn
for those castle walls.
too thick,
too stuffy,
where it is
is not where it should be.
the strands through
your scalp come from
an ancient riddle of rising
above and extending beyond,
my dear Rapunzel.

You should know this story
was never a blank page,
it was always stained
with color, this ruin
is what made it perfect,
when you look outside
of your barred windows,
don't starry skies resemble
your story— a black sea
stained with bright lights,
isn't it beautiful?

One day you'll take your
place where you belong
amongst this Milky Way,
flying on the clouds
of your hair that was never
meant for a castle without doors—
      was meant for the Suns and the Moons,
      meant for the Neptunes and the Jupiters,
      for the Nebulas and the Supernovas,
meant to fly little my starlight,
meant to fly.

VI

Ascension

and someone said dead roses weren't pretty,
told me i wasn't beautiful

CINDERELLA'S BROKEN FOOT

She fears her sisters in the wall,
becoming a horrendous woman,
this gorgeous child then committed
to an eternity of walking on glass.

Trauma refracting through footprints,
perhaps, survival's enduring inside a flask,
the ladies throw stones on her way to church,
yet, she fears her sisters in the wall.

Princes beg her to *heel*,
the shoe does not fit,
she wears it,
fears becoming the sisters in the wall.

Lady Liberty despises injustice,
she breaks the sword of her tongue,
moving to a glass house,
with her sisters in the wall.

Feet blistered and bruised,
a rolled ankle shatters her sole,
tears withdraw, *won't cry*
not by the sisters in the wall.

A medic brings stitches,
she asks, *can he fix a glass shoe?*
wear it or burn it, he says,
"You are not your sisters in the wall."

ANCESTRAL ECHOES

Brown Skin is Baritone and Soprano,
(((*Our Brown Has Sound*)))

Brown like autumn leaves,
but we don't fall easy,
we just breeze.

Like you, my little Brown girl,
on that warm Palm Sunday
be's at ease.

"Don't cry before service," they said,
and we thought you'd hold it in,
but you can't hold brown.
— *we kinda the shit!*

And that's on your Father's shirt,
couldn't explain why we were late to church,
but *it was written,*
all on our different shades of brown,

You, my little brown girl,
have the crown.
Carried, escorted, and served free meals,
"Hey y'all, the new girl's in town!"

And your family's men honor in artistic ways,
so if you're ever lost, be not ashamed,
Cry!
For your cry brought us together,
and remember Brown girl,
we Yoruba is no quiet people,

(((*Our Brown Has Sound*)))

A LINEAGE OF SURVIVORS

"Breathe boy . . . Breathe,"

His father said.

Reminded that living

is not automatic,

that life is the jewel

beneath the cave,

mined and discovered.

His baby was born

atop an open rebellion,

birthed into the stolen wind,

conceived with lavender lungs.

"Breathe boy . . . Breathe,"

His father said,

overcome the quiet whisper,

give no home to the suffering,

find the jewel beneath the cave,

discover it,

"Breathe boy . . . breathe . . . fight!"

His father said.

BEAUTY & THE SORROW

He likes to dance.
He likes to forget
these walls have eyes
and the floorboards
ears listening to his music.
He likes to forget spite
and wear his nose first,
allowing his feet to walk by faith
abandoning his limited sight.
Only sound—
only rhythm,
& blues.
And he likes to forget
the vibrations in the hall,
Tuesday's fingernail on records,
ski-skip-skipping his favorite tracks.
he remembers the guru's meditation
from previous chapter's detox,
the party was always inside,
the ticket is letting go.
Allowing hips to roll,
       arms to wave,
       sweat to drop,
       and toes to fly.
A shame the world
will only see the rain,
but not the man
dancing on the sky.

BAPTIZED IN FIRE

You taught me how to pray.
It was the only thing I knew
that kept you close
when others kept us far.
Perhaps this truth is blasphemous,
but *this truth* is important than sacrilege,
— I need you to know. . .
my faith was filled with maggots,
smelled of embalming solutions
coating a weeping corpse.
Ashes, urns, and abandoned churches,
below living temperature thresholds,
and this casket of an existence
was once my absolute truth.

They say there is power in the tongue,
so one day I exercised this muscle,
and learned that there's a fireplace,
a warm memory encoded through language,
where God (haven't said that in a while)
communes with strangers
like it was *His* last supper.
Believing in something
greater than death,
believing in
Our Ascension.

Some say there is
power in belief,
Truth is
I don't really know yet. . .
But I believe in *You,*
so maybe,
it is true.

WHEN YOU GET OLDER

"Find us,"
that's all a puzzle can ask.

See the family picture
behind a *purple world,*
the shadows in the dark,
nightingales & mages—
it all begins in *the attic.*
I hate that so many
windows closed,
that we may wait
until you get older
to play games
made for a child.
But we were born
human— born broken,
born *hurting someone*
that pushed for us,
forced to find faith
at the *end of the tunnel.*
we had to earn hope,
claw and battle for the
right to *walk,*
but love may indeed
grow into *family trees*
if we make peace
with our choices, you see?
See the picture through
the *sisters on the wall,*
hear the *sons of winter*
laughing in *The Night*—

        "Find us,"
that's all a puzzle can ask.

i love you
as an umbrella
loves the sunrise

ACKNOWLEDGEMENTS

This book is based on true events of my life that affected my family, my faith and my morality. I'd like to take a moment to thank those that have contributed to the manifestation of this art which has assisted in the development of myself, as I've become a better writer, a better philosopher, and a better man.

To my older brother, *the man who raised the torch*, Olutola Gaiusbayode, thank you for sacrificing your youth to see our family survive. Thank you for still being a father to your daughter despite the obstacles that have broken and destroyed other men. You raised me in a household, during the absence of our parents, when you were still a child learning about life, love, adulthood, and perseverance. You provided leadership rooted in intellectual thought which inspired the introspection necessary for me to write this book.

To the Self-Publishing School and my editor T. Lesfargues, thank you for providing me with tools and understanding that has helped me actualize this dream of a project.

To poets, writers, and artists that have inspired me along the way, from writers of the past like Langston Hughes, Shel Silverstein, Dylan Thomas, and Gwendolyn Brooks to modern poets like Tripp Fontane, Amaria Jones, Atlas The Poet, Caroline Bennett, Jayson Reynolds, and so many more — I am grateful.

To my lifelong mentor, Malik Willoughby, I am grateful for your spirituality, calm, and balance that helped me meditate on the rage dwelling inside of me when I was separated from my niece. When I would studied in college, her picture would be on my desk and the thought of not being able to call her, see her, or tell her I love her broke my heart. Thank you for providing the necessary *detoxes* for me to heal.

To my friends that have known of my suffering, and to the many that have not, thank you for existing in my life and providing spaces of joy.

To the lover that was my *Aral Sea*, thank you for your providing a love that created a space for me to just "be"; I wish you the utmost peace and prosperity. To my college roommate Cameron Rucker, my brother, my best friend, thank you for being a shoulder I have leaned on when traversing these family struggles.

To my niece, *my little ladybug, my little starlight*, Scarlett. . . girl, I love you so much. You are my first niece. You taught me how to love and how to pray because both actions are choices that were tested in my darkest times. I'm sorry there were days I didn't know how to love you or playfight with you because I was wrestling with the emotional trauma of our family's circumstance. I'm sorry that you had to bear the weight of your parents' relationship when you were only five years old, and you would cry in your father's arms telling him how much it hurts. I'm sorry your other side kept you away from us. I hope that after reading this book, my words assist you in finding peace, truth and understanding through the challenges of your life. You are a remarkable young girl and will become a brilliant woman when you get older. I already see the glimpses of your exceptionality when we chill and talk. So, from me to you, whenever you need something, know that you have a family that will care for you, love for you, and fight for you. We've had to before, through winter and through storm, we will do it again. No matter the time. Through the day, and through *The Night*.
We are here.
We are real.

Peace and love kiddo,
Your favorite uncle (*don't tell the other guys. . .*)

www.ingramcontent.com/pod-product-compliance
Lightning Source LLC
Chambersburg PA
CBHW032037040426
42449CB00007B/923